W9-BGQ-535

It's a Goal!

Written by Claire Owen

Brazil

My name is Rafael, and I live in Rio de Janeiro, Brazil. My favorite sport is soccer. Did you know that soccer is called *football* in Brazil and many other countries? What sport do you think of when you hear the word *football*?

Contents

Country of Champions   4

An Ancient Game   6

Record Crowds   8

On the Field   10

Football Shapes   12

The World Cup   14

Finals Fever   16

Amazing Audiences   18

Women's Soccer   20

For Richer or Poorer   22

Sample Answers   24

Index   24

Wherever you see me, you'll find activities to try and questions to answer.

Country of Champions

If you ask a soccer fan where the best players in the world come from, the answer is likely to be "Brazil!" Soccer, or *futebol*, as it is called in Brazil, is the country's most popular sport. It is played everywhere—from large stadiums to sandy beaches and small clearings in the jungle. Brazil has produced some of the finest teams and players of all time, including the legendary Pelé.

Edson Arantes do Nascimento, nicknamed Pelé, is considered by many people to be the greatest soccer player of all time. During a career lasting more than two decades, Pelé scored 1,281 goals in 1,363 games.

Soccer clubs around the world are always on the lookout for the next superstar from Brazil. In 2005, several clubs, including England's Manchester United, competed to sign up Jean Carlos Chera (right), who was only nine years old!

An Ancient Game

Games that involve kicking or throwing a ball have been played for thousands of years. In England, football was popular from about the eighth century, but it was a very different game from that which is played today. Early games of football often involved hundreds of people and could last all day. By 1863, two very different sets of rules had developed, and the sport was split into rugby and Association Football, or soccer. Today, soccer has 250 million registered players in more than 200 countries and is the world's largest spectator sport.

Rugby is thought to date back to 1823, when a student at Rugby School in England took the ball in his arms and ran with it.

Did You Know?

Soccer was introduced into Brazil in 1890 by Charles Miller, a young man who had returned home from school in England.

spectator sport a sport watched, both live and on television, by large numbers of fans

Football has come to mean different things in different parts of the world. In England, Europe, and South America, it refers to soccer. In the United States, it means American football or gridiron. In Australia, it refers to a fast and exciting game played by "Australian Rules."

How many years ago was the split between rugby and soccer? How many years later was soccer introduced into Brazil?

Record Crowds

Brazilians love to watch soccer, so it is just as well that the world's largest stadium is in Rio de Janeiro! The Maracanã was built for the 1950 World Cup, which was hosted by Brazil. A crowd of 199,854 people watched the final match, which Brazil lost 2–1 to Uruguay. According to the *Guinness Book of World Records*, this was the largest crowd ever to watch a sporting event.

Some Record Football Crowds

Sport	Location	No. of Spectators
Soccer	Glasgow, Scotland, 1937	149,547
Australian Rules	Melbourne, Australia, 1970	121,696
Rugby	Sydney, Australia, 2000	109,874

Pick a number on this page. How much greater than that number was the record crowd at the Maracanã in 1950?

America's largest football stadium (above), Michigan Stadium, University of Michigan, has a seating capacity of 107,501 spectators. This makes it slightly larger than Beaver Stadium, Penn State University (106,537), and Neyland Stadium, University of Tennessee (104,079).

capacity   the amount of space that can be filled

On the Field

Soccer is played on a rectangular field. For international matches, the length of the field may vary from a minimum of 110 yards to a maximum of 120 yards. The width of the field must be no narrower than 70 yards and no wider than 80 yards. Women and juniors usually play on a smaller field. In fact, for six-year-olds, the field may be as small as 25 yards by 15 yards!

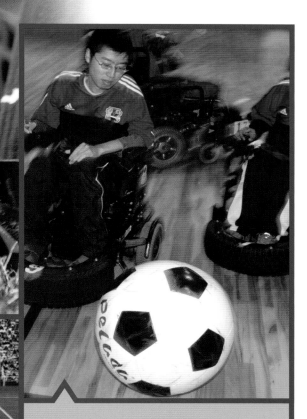

Wheelchair soccer, called power soccer, is played indoors, on a smaller "field" but with a much larger ball.

Football Fields Around the World

- A rugby field is up to 110 yards long and 75 yards wide.

- An American football field is 120 yards long and 160 feet wide.

- Australian Rules is played on an oval ground up to about 200 yards long and 170 yards wide.

Figure It Out

1. If you had to buy sod for each of the following fields, how many square feet would you need?

   a. the smallest soccer field for international matches

   b. the largest soccer field for international matches

   c. the largest rugby field

   d. an American football field

2. Calculate the length of the chalk line (in feet) drawn around each of the fields in question 1.

3. How many square feet are equivalent to one square yard? Convert your answers for question 1 into square yards.

4. Copy and complete these sentences.

   a. The area of the largest soccer field is _____ square yards more than the area of an American football field.

   b. The area of the largest soccer field is _____ times greater than the area of an American football field.

Football Shapes

A soccer ball is similar in shape to a polyhedron called a *truncated icosahedron*. Both are made from the same *net*, or arrangement, of hexagons and pentagons, but a soccer ball is inflated to form a sphere. Officially, a soccer ball measures 27 to 28 inches in circumference and weighs between 14 and 16 ounces.

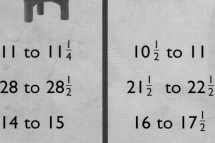

Using data from this chart, make up a problem for a partner to solve.

In other versions of football, the ball is an egg shape called an *ellipsoid*.

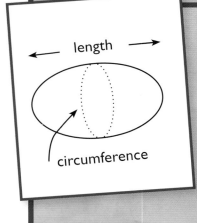

length

circumference

	Rugby	**American Football**	**Australian Rules**
	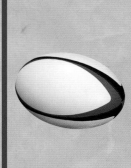		
Length (in.)	$10\frac{3}{4}$ to $11\frac{1}{2}$	11 to $11\frac{1}{4}$	$10\frac{1}{2}$ to 11
Circumference (in.)	23 to 24	28 to $28\frac{1}{2}$	$21\frac{1}{2}$ to $22\frac{1}{2}$
Weight (oz)	$13\frac{1}{2}$ to $15\frac{1}{2}$	14 to 15	16 to $17\frac{1}{2}$

polyhedron   a three-dimensional shape with faces that are polygons

Make a Truncated Icosahedron

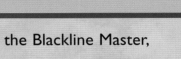

You will need two card-stock copies of the Blackline Master, scissors, and clear tape.

1. Cut out the 10 groups of 3 or 4 hexagons and pentagons.

2. Tape the groups together to create a net like the one below.

3. Put a crease along every line where two shapes join together.

4. Fold up the polyhedron and tape the nearby edges together.

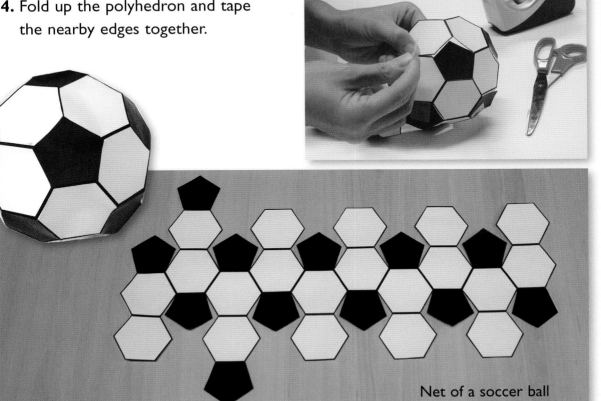

Net of a soccer ball

The World Cup

The World Cup is the most important competition in international soccer. World Cup finals have been held every four years since 1930, except for 1942 and 1946. The actual competition for the cup begins two years before the finals. In each of six regions around the world, countries compete for a much-sought-after place in the finals.

After the announcement that South Africa would host the 2010 World Cup, former President Nelson Mandela was photographed holding the World Cup trophy.

How many times has the World Cup been held?

World Cup Statistics

	1994	1998	2002
Host Country	U.S.A.	France	Japan & Korea
Qualification Tournament			
Participating countries	147	174	193
Matches played	497	643	777
Goals scored	1,431	1,922	2,452
Finals Tournament			
Participating countries	24	32	32
Matches played	52	64	64
Goals scored	141	171	161
Number of spectators	3,587,088	2,775,400	2,705,566

For the three competitions above, use averages to compare the number of goals scored and the number of spectators per match.

Did You Know?

- Brazil is the only nation to have qualified for the finals in every World Cup ever held.

- Brazil has won the World Cup five times. No other country has won more than three times.

Finals Fever

Only 13 teams participated in the first World Cup finals, held in Uruguay in 1930. From 1934 to 1978, there were 16 teams in each finals competition. The number of finalists was increased to 24 teams in 1982 and to 32 teams in 1998. For the first round of the finals, the 32 teams are divided into eight groups of four. Each team plays each of the other teams in that group.

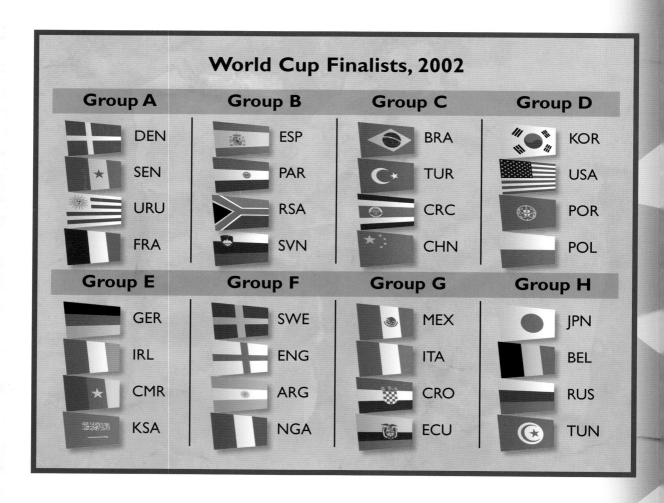

World Cup Finalists, 2002

Group A	Group B	Group C	Group D
DEN	ESP	BRA	KOR
SEN	PAR	TUR	USA
URU	RSA	CRC	POR
FRA	SVN	CHN	POL

Group E	Group F	Group G	Group H
GER	SWE	MEX	JPN
IRL	ENG	ITA	BEL
CMR	ARG	CRO	RUS
KSA	NGA	ECU	TUN

World Cup Finals Competitions

- First-round matches
- Second-round matches
- 4 quarter-finals
- 2 semi-finals
- Final for third place
- Final

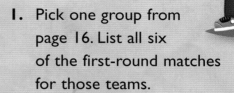

Figure It Out

1. Pick one group from page 16. List all six of the first-round matches for those teams.

2. Altogether, how many matches are played in the first round?

3. In the first round, teams score 3 points for a win, 1 point for a draw, and 0 points for a loss. How many points did Brazil and the United States score in 2002?

Brazil	vs.	Turkey	2–1
Brazil	vs.	China	4–0
Costa Rica	vs.	Brazil	2–5
U.S.A.	vs.	Portugal	3–2
Korea	vs.	U.S.A.	1–1
Poland	vs.	U.S.A.	3–1

4. In the second round, the top team from each group plays the second team from another group.

   a. How many teams compete in the second round?

   b. How many matches are played in the second round?

5. How many matches in all are played in the World Cup finals?

Amazing Audiences

The top soccer events attract huge television audiences around the world. The 2002 World Cup final between Brazil and Germany, for example, attracted more than 1.1 billion viewers worldwide. The total number of viewers for all of the matches combined was more than 28.8 billion! Rugby and football also attract large, worldwide TV audiences. Australian Rules, on the other hand, has much smaller audiences, as it is watched mainly by people from Australia.

Some Record Television Audiences

Did You Know?

Advertisers paid $1,085,000 for a 30-second commercial slot during Super Bowl XXX.

Rugby

2003 World Cup
Opening Ceremony
1 billion viewers worldwide

World population: 6 billion

Australian Rules

AFL Grand Final, 2003
3.5 million Australian viewers

Australia's population:
19.9 million

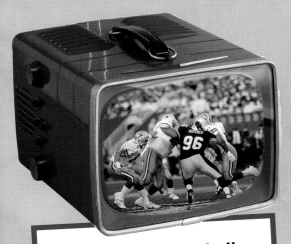

American Football

Super Bowl XXX
January 28, 1996
138.5 million U.S. viewers

U.S. population: 265 million

For each of the events on this page, use a calculator to find the audience as a percent of the population. Discuss the results.

Women's Soccer

In England, women's soccer became popular during World War I, and a women's match in 1920 attracted a crowd of 53,000 spectators. The following year, the Football Association decided that "the game of football is quite unsuitable for females and ought not to be encouraged." It was not until the 1970s that this ban on women was lifted. Since then, women's soccer has become one of the world's fastest-growing sports.

Women's soccer became an Olympic sport in 1996, and the women's World Cup has been held every four years since 1991.

World Cup Finals

1991 U.S.A. vs. Norway (2–1)
1995 Norway vs. Germany (2–0)
1999 U.S.A. vs. China (0–0)
2003 Germany vs. Sweden (2–1)

Olympic Finals

1996 U.S.A. vs. China (2–1)
2000 Norway vs. U.S.A. (3–2)
2004 U.S.A. vs. Brazil (2–1)

In which of these years will a women's World Cup be held? Which of these are Olympic years?
A. 2013 B. 2018
C. 2023 D. 2024
E. 2039

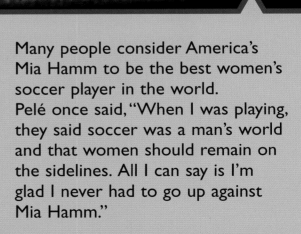

Many people consider America's Mia Hamm to be the best women's soccer player in the world. Pelé once said, "When I was playing, they said soccer was a man's world and that women should remain on the sidelines. All I can say is I'm glad I never had to go up against Mia Hamm."

For Richer or Poorer

Soccer is a sport that can be played by anyone, rich or poor. Children in a small African village, for example, need only a ball to be able to enjoy a game of soccer. At the other extreme, wealthy soccer clubs in England and Europe pay huge fees to get the best players to transfer to their teams, and they charge high prices for soccer merchandise. Some of these clubs have a turnover of more than $200,000,000 per year.

turnover   the total revenue from goods and services

22

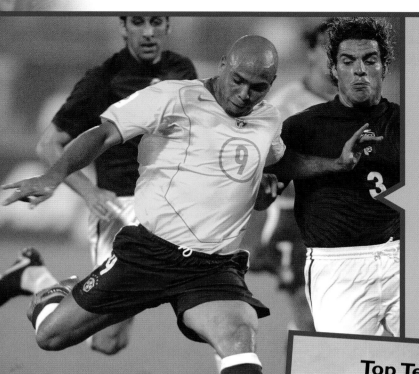

Brazil's Ronaldo is one of the world's most expensive players. After being paid a transfer fee of $55.8 million in 2002, he transferred again in 2003 for $21.9 million.

Top Ten Transfer Fees

Year	Player (Birthplace)	Fee (Millions)
1999	Vieri (Italy)	52.9
2000	Crespo (Argentina)	70.1
2000	Figo (Portugal)	76.6
2001	Costa (Portugal)	54.2
2001	Inzaghi (Italy)	51.1
2001	Mendieta (Spain)	59.5
2001	Veron (Argentina)	57.5
2001	Zidane (France)	93.2
2002	Ferdinand (England)	58.1
2002	Ronaldo (Brazil)	55.8

List the transfer fees in order, from greatest to least. What is the difference between the greatest fee and each of the other fees?

Sample Answers

Find out the dimensions of a hockey field or basketball court. Compare its perimeter and area with those of the largest soccer field for international matches.

Page 9   50,307; 78,158; 89,980; 92,353; 93,317; 95,775

Page 11   1. a. 69,300 sq. ft
                          b. 86,400 sq. ft
                          c. 74,250 sq. ft   d. 57,600 sq. ft

               2. a. 1,080 ft   b. 1,200 ft
                          c. 1,110 ft   d. 1,040 ft

               3. 9 sq. ft. a. 7,700 sq. yd b. 9,600 sq. yd
                          c. 8,250 sq. yd   d. 6,400 sq. yd

               4. a. 3,200 sq. yd   b. $1\frac{1}{2}$

Page 14   18 times (up to 2006)

Page 15   Goals: 2.88, 2.99, 3.16 (Qual.);
               2.71, 2.67, 2.52 (Finals)
               Spectators: 68,982; 43,366; 42,274

Page 17   2. 48 matches

               3. Brazil: 9 points; U.S.A.: 4 points

               4. a. 16 teams   b. 8 matches

               5. 64 matches (48+8+4+2+1+1)

Page 19   Rugby: about 17%; Australian Rules: about 18%; American Football: about 52%

Page 21   C, E; D

Page 23   93.2, 76.6, 70.1, 59.5, 58.1, 57.5, 55.8, 54.2, 52.9, 51.1; 16.6, 23.1, 33.7, 35.1, 35.7, 37.4, 39.0, 40.3, 42.1

Index

American football   7, 9, 11–12, 18–19
Australian Rules   7, 9, 11–12, 18–19
rugby   6–7, 9, 11–12, 18–19
soccer   4–12, 14–18, 20–23
women's soccer   20–21
World Cup (soccer)   8–9, 14–18, 21